FUN AND GAMES

Recess

Problem Solving

Dona Herweck Rice

Consultants

Colene Van Brunt
Math Coach
Hillsborough County Public Schools

Publishing Credits

Rachelle Cracchiolo, M.S.Ed., *Publisher*
Conni Medina, M.A.Ed., *Managing Editor*
Dona Herweck Rice, *Series Developer*
Emily R. Smith, M.A.Ed., *Series Developer*
Diana Kenney, M.A.Ed., NBCT, *Content Director*
June Kikuchi, *Content Director*
Susan Daddis, M.A.Ed., *Editor*
Karen Malaska, M.Ed., *Editor*
Kevin Panter, *Senior Graphic Designer*

Image Credits: pp.18–19 Mitchell Funk/Getty Images; all other images from iStock and/or Shutterstock.

Library of Congress Cataloging-in-Publication Data

Names: Rice, Dona, author.
Title: Fun and games : recess / Dona Herweck Rice.
Other titles: Recess
Description: Huntington Beach, CA : Teacher Created Materials, 2019. |
  Includes index. | Audience: K to Grade 3. |
Identifiers: LCCN 2017054963 (print) | LCCN 2018008160 (ebook) | ISBN
  9781480759787 (eBook) | ISBN 9781425856847 (pbk.)
Subjects: LCSH: School recess breaks--Juvenile literature. | Problem
  solving--Juvenile literature.
Classification: LCC LB3033 (ebook) | LCC LB3033 .R53 2019 (print) | DDC
  371.2/44--dc23
LC record available at https://lccn.loc.gov/2017054963

Teacher Created Materials

5301 Oceanus Drive
Huntington Beach, CA 92649-1030
www.tcmpub.com

ISBN 978-1-4258-5684-7

Table of Contents

Hooray!

Hooray, hooray!

It is time to play!

It is time to go to **recess** today!

Many kids think recess is the **best** time of the school day.

What do you think?

Great Things about Recess

Recess is a time to be with friends.

It is a time to go outside and play.

There are 6 kids playing tag. There are 4 kids playing hopscotch. There are 8 kids playing ball. How many total kids are playing?

1. Draw or place objects on ten frames to solve the problem.

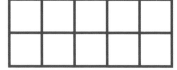

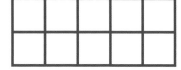

2. Write an equation to show your thinking.

Inside the school, students must sit still.

They must be **quiet**.

At recess, they can move and shout!

They can play on the playground and blacktop.

What to Do

There is a lot to do outside on the playground.

Some kids like to **swing**. Other kids like to **slide**.

Some kids like to jump rope on the blacktop.

Other kids like to kick balls on the grass.

Ms. Ruiz's class has 4 jump ropes, 5 kickballs, and 3 footballs to play with at recess.

1. How many total toys does the class have? Solve on a number line. Write an equation to show your thinking.

2. Ms. Ruiz has 20 students. How many more toys does she need for each student to have a toy? How do you know?

Some kids like to walk around the playground.

Other kids like to talk to their friends.

Something for Everyone

Recess has games and fun for everyone!

What do you like to do?

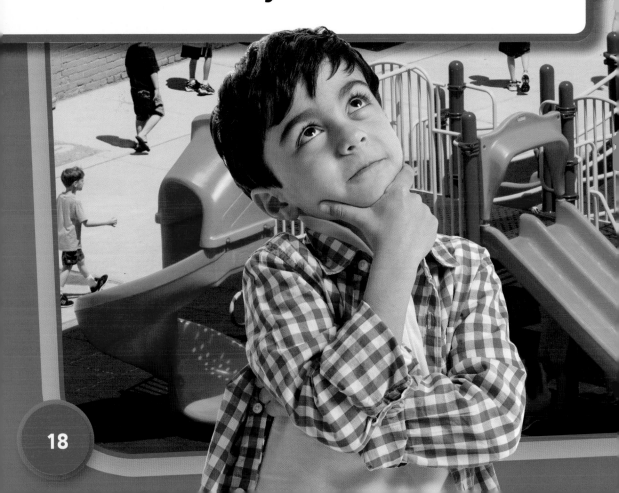

Christopher likes to play different games at recess. He plays kickball for 4 minutes. He plays football for 6 minutes. He jumps rope for 7 minutes.

How long does Christopher play at recess? Solve on an open number line. Write an equation to show your thinking.

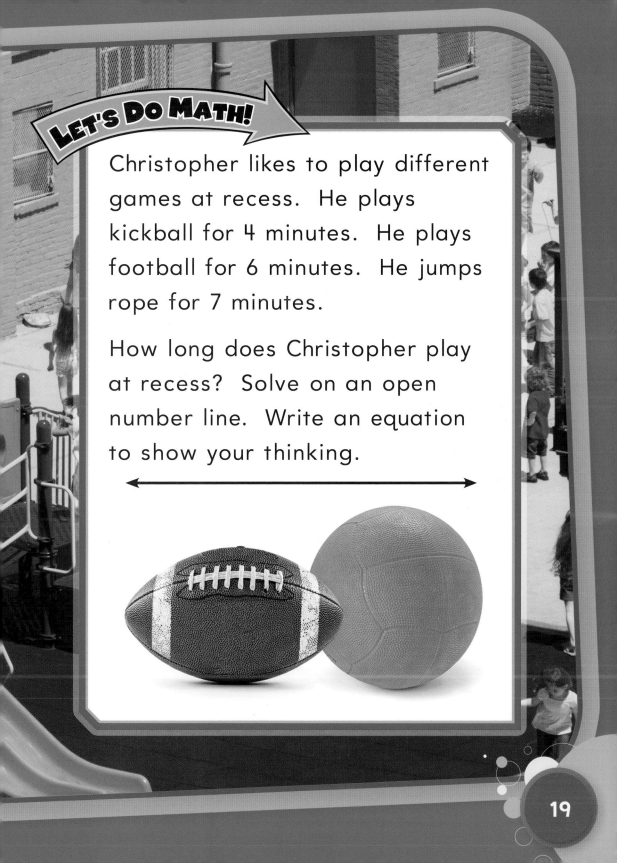

⚙️ Problem Solving

It is recess time. Everyone wants to play. Draw the missing picture. Write the missing equation.

Word Problem	Pictures	Equation
1. A class has 1 ball, 6 ropes, and 8 hoops. How many toys does the class have?		1 + 6 + 8 = ___
2. 8 students play tag, 2 jump rope, and 3 play ball. How many students are playing?		

Glossary

best—favorite

hooray—a happy cheer

quiet—no noise

recess—outdoor time during the
school day

slide—to go down a ramp

swing—to go back and forth on a
moving seat

Index

Answer Key

Let's Do Math!

page 9:

1. 18 kids

2. $6 + 4 + 8 = 18$

page 15:

1. 12 toys

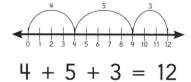

$4 + 5 + 3 = 12$

2. 8 more toys are needed. Answers will vary but may include using a number line.

page 19:

17 minutes; Number lines and equations will vary. Example:

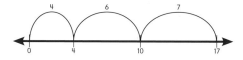

$4 + 6 + 7 = 17$

Problem Solving

1. 15; Pictures will vary.

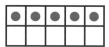

2. $8 + 2 + 3 = 13$